# Crow Song

*To Joyce –*
*With every good wish !*
*Zoe Keithley*
*10.03.10*

# ZOE KEITHLEY

Roan Press
Sacramento, California
2009

*Crow Song* ©2009, Roan Press
ISBN 0-9815968-2-7

Roan Press
Sacramento's Small Literary Publisher
P.O. Box 160406
Sacramento, CA 95816
roanpress@gmail.com

www.roanpress.com

Printed in California

Cover photo courtesy of Getty Images

Book design by The California Poet Productions:
thecaliforniapoet@yahoo.com

Printing by Sierra Office Supply and Printing

## ACKNOWLEDGEMENTS

Many of the following poems were performed with *World Enough and Time*, a poetry/music ensemble that appeared at university, college, church, radio, festival, small theater and nightclub events over a period of fifteen years in the greater Chicago area, Indiana and Wisconsin, and were also published in performance chapbooks and on videotape over those years. In addition, "We Pity the Monkey" appeared as "Organ Grinder" in *Unity Magazine*. "Visit from a Maenad" won top honors in the Adult Division of the annual Poetry Competition of the Evanston Public Library, Evanston, IL.

I wish to extend my heartfelt thanks to Brad Buchanan for his wonderful editorial eye and to Roan Press for choosing *Crow Song* as an offering. I also wish to acknowledge Carolyn Kelley Williams, Kathy Kelly Hahn, and *World Enough and Time* for fifteen years of shared performances in the midwest during which time many of the poems in this collection were written and aired.

To Liz, Clare and Chris.
To Fiona. To Ian.

# TABLE OF CONTENTS

## III/ Scavenging

## IV/ The Long Iridescent Flight

# PROLOGUE

# Crow Song

Mid-morning. I look up from my desk to see the crows
settle at the rim of the large elm across the alley,
full-grown and suited in silk. Orange sun bounds
from their bodies. As they face one another, heads low
and necks elongated like geese, they push the blades
of their wings skyward to scissor into the beating air
an intricate and fabulous design of greeting.
From where I sit, they could be mirrored twins
in this elegant and ageless ceremony, solemn yet alive
with desire. All is over by a count of three. At some
discreet signal, then, they pitch out wing tip to wing tip
to sail above my window in perfect and unhurried ease.

I wish you had been there as they clipped their meaning
into that sky. I saw live origami, saw them proffer
as nobility does that ancient ceremony of homage three times,
quick as finger snaps; but with a swelling of joy that stirred
the very molecules in the flagstone and furniture below.
I know I felt the energetic shift, awe-struck at how my eye
sprang from my work the instant they settled upon that tree,
as if I too belonged in this scene. Then they were gone,
and left behind a shock of emptiness to ring down
the alley and in me.

Hours later I came to wonder if you had sent them.
It would not be the first time birds had come to me.
I want to think that, at some signal telegraphed
in silence, you made visible this way a fresh agreement
between our hearts. I want to think that leaping
every dimension including the slow grind of thought,
scattering a soup of lightless air and streaking like falling stars
between two worlds, we meet like these crows to bow
low, to lift our wings and, in a twin movement, scissor
into this space widening within our minds a blaze
of happy recognition.

3

# I/ CIRCLING

## Morning Light

Leaf tips raised to fire.
The familiar breeze, like a cat,
brushes the marked green spears.
Clusters of infant fruit
shine female under the brooding canopy.
Behind them, the thick trunk gnarls upward
mounted by the ravening ivy.
My own yearning rushes out to meet me.
The beloved is everywhere.

## My mouth is filled

                                          with the grasses
the creature has eaten. I taste them green
in its tissue, tear them as this beast did
once from the soil, inhale them rising
delicious from the flesh, devour them
in the great flanks they have built.
We, the many mouths and teeth, are
one in this: eating beauty so it does not die.

## Sunlight Slants Across the Sill

It slants across the wall in 313,
Foreman High School, lights the cord
moving in the open window. I sit
near, wanting air, to be outdoors,
beyond the parking lot below,
at the running track where boys
and girls sprint and walk, sprint
and walk. The eye of the track is
emerald, the grass up fresh from winter
sleep. Beyond it, trees reach tall
and flame with leaf buds. Scraps
of clouds drift east. My eye follows
an older man and woman, out of place,
come over from the neighborhood to stroll
the center of the lawn, winter coats
thrown wide, feet synchronized,
heads bent in conversation.
Around them, this necklace of life.
But their focus is on one another,
on the subject between them.
They carry the peace, affection,
and patience in their gait
of old and timeless friends.
They crown the morning.

## In those folk clubs

of the fifties and sixties,
we'd be crammed around these tiny dark tables
all covered with wet glass rings and beer bottles
to peer through the sheets of smoke hanging between us
and the postage stamp stage where the bass player
teeters on a corner thumping up and down
while the singer-guy who's not that much older
than we are wears a crew cut and a skinny black tie
and bangs away at his banjo warbling out pictures
of sparkling oceans and golden valleys or being stuck
in Terre Haute and loving the wrong woman or losing
your money or your life or your dog Blue in Albuquerque
while traveling on through this old world of woe.
We'd scarf French fries and onion rings, guzzle
too much beer, laugh and cry and sing along
loud and full, shout for "More, more," our lives ripening
on the great luxurious bough so leafy and green.


(for Bob Gibson)

# Philosophy I

light within blazing
light without blazing
we dance
prisoners of glory

## We pity the monkey

but whoever considers the organ grinder,
how he loves his music to distraction,
is in heaven with all that melody rushing
out from under his fingers, filling him up
until he must burst into song?

Did you ever think perhaps the monkey
comes with the organ, and the grinder
must put up with it if he wants the music?
If he wants the music he must tolerate
the high jinks, the posturing, the running
in circles—all for the love of his art.
And add insult to injury, the monkey
tipping his cap and begging for quarters
as if it were someone else's idea.

## Northern California December

Outside the motel room, the loud wet slap
of melting snow against the sidewalk below.
We turn, drugged with sleep, to knit
more deeply again into one another's arms
while high above the weather-beaten roofs
of this small town, our Mother Shasta spreads
wide her white and ancient cloak to brood
warm over every dreaming nest and lair,
over every branch, bed and burrow.

## To reach the ocean


you must first pass along CA 152
and so through the woman sleeping as if upon her side
and all her embellishments open and in shameless display;
and coming on like an avalanche toward your speeding car.
But then, it is her quarters through which you pass
and upon which you intrude, so if she wishes you to see
how the last light of day crawls across her breasts, clings
to what of her is round while it also feels its way along dark
and secret crevices, or to reveal what she idly cups sweet
and wanton, or how she lets the silken water plunge
cool over her extremities, who is to stop her? You forget
the ocean, the motel, the lover you are to meet, your name,
your useless skin rumpled upon the seat beside you
to open fins of fingers and feet to stroke the thick honey light
until, viscous and thinning, you too flow over her,
spilling, clinging, coating; and rise slowly, slowly
until you have become that very air cradling her.

## Quetico Provincial Park, Canada

All those green trees
and dishes of blue water,
brown fish under our canoe,
back and forth.
There is peace in the sunlight,
in these dense woods.
We eat what we catch,
drink pure sweetness from the lake.
At night we hear the loon
go crazy, then bring silence down,
smell the kindness of the trees
in the pine boughs overhead
where the whiskey jack sleeps.
There is peace in the white moon
as it rocks upon the water,
and in this shining black lake,
in this liquid air bathing us,
infusing a birthright that we forget
is ours as well.

## With luck

you find the elusive notch where
water has ground a path through the base
of the mountain. First, the narrow passage
wide enough for a canoe; next, glide
into the vaulting caves, into room after
watery room to a silence that pacifies
the bones and is broken only by soft lapping
and the shutter of bird wings diving from a high perch.
The air is cool and makes the stones radiate as soft colors
of woodlands beyond. Here at last is safety and peace;
here places within you so far unmapped. They call.

## Bobbing on the bough

                   small and hard
but green with promise, the pippin is sustained.
But it is not the tree that ripens its fruit.
Possibility is all a tree can offer, and hope.
Instead it is the pippin's giving up of its thousand
microscopic orifices to the heat and excitement
of the sun's radiance that grows, cell by cell,
the lavish tissue and blushing skin. Such a mating
of heaven and earth, such surrender and permeation
creates this swell of love whose flesh we divide
between us now beneath this tree where vistas
of the world spread before us. I turn from the sight
of the trembling blue hills to your waiting arms,
breathe deep your perfume, trace with my tongue
the perfect scroll of your ear. What you are seeps
softly into my most secret places where ecstasy wakes
each membrane. It is this way you become
flesh of my flesh; and daily I too ripen, lavish and fragrant,
while the running juice of this wholly intercourse
rises in glistening beads to stand openly upon my skin.

## For a Fellow Traveler

I spot you far ahead,
a tiny speck, rounding a ridge.
I wave, but you do not see
me still trudging the valley,
the distance too great for the gesture.
Perhaps we will meet
farther along the trail at some clearing
where progress has given you
space for rest and vista to observe
the path you have been over.
We might share a tin of coffee then
and swap stories of the road:
How the heat of the day makes the sweat roll
and unforgiving stones trouble the calves;
funny and wonderful fellow travelers,
knapsacks and burros, all going the same way,
their strange kindnesses or unexpected gifts;
as well as those from creature world:
The hostel of a sudden stream
or, harvest to hand, sweet juice
of wild strawberries waiting
deep in a secret wood;
at night the silent companionship
of the stars
witnessing other constellations of light
glowing within us.
May hunger, for us all, end in strawberries;
and thirst at the loving lip of a lake.
May the heat of the day swell every cell
until it pours forth gold.
And may whatever wind ruffles our hair
turn, and turn
until it comes from the south.

# II/ FROM THE NEST

## Fish

I am
restless
curious of the deep

some subterranean pig
routing corner and crevice
for pearl
for bloodstone
for deep blue diamond

I
fish
hunting
and
hunted

amen

## Lilacs, Isabelle,

and small birds springing
from the grass, singing;
a full moon on a summer's night,
butterflies lighting space
between the trees and a soft
musing melody whispered
through the reeds. All these
I steal to show you yourself.


(for my mother)

# 5021 Drexel Boulevard

I remember grandpa at dinner, ready to carve,
stern behind his mustache and vest; the candles
smoking. And light pouring onto the sun porch
breakfast table where the pulp of my first orange
juice clung to my teeth like wet rags. I remember
the broad quiet sidewalk outside hot with sunlight
and splashed with shade of the slender dignified trees,
nursemaids of the neighborhood; the drinking fountain
hooded like a monk chattering in diamond-bright
syllables endlessly—and always on a merry subject—
all summer long.

I remember the grand fountain that crowned
Drexel Boulevard was our wading pool. Curtains
of water woven of soft beads of sky-blue, sun-orange,
deep rose spilled in a happy rush over the curved
metal lips of four giant green shells. I remember
little heads like skeins of thread bobbed, uproarious,
in the sparkling light and other eyes the same size
as my own joy-filled as the water; tiny buds of nipples
and little dark umbilical caves, all of interesting shapes.

I remember the satin caress of the self-replenishing fountain
that could never get enough of feeling us, sliding
its silken hands everyplace: holding us, letting us go,
holding us again, never tiring of kissing us. Oh, it made
us bold to be so loved. Summer after summer, the fountain
gave its delicious water to surprise our hot skin, and,
holding within the scope of its wide arms all our healthy
shouts, whispered into our cells its laws of generosity
and discipline and its welcome of us human creatures.

Driving Drexel Boulevard yesterday toward the fountain,
as surely as if my mother's cheek had brushed mine, your
spirit, glowing from you, caught at my heart before my eyes
ever saw you battered, the graceful black filigree ironwork

of your front door torn open, elegant ebony canopy scuffed
and warped; and your friends across the street no better off,
their proud faces scarred, blistered, teeth broken out—
eyes some places blind as boards.

You'd think, coming back like this, I'd be enraged.
But I wasn't. I know lies when I see them.
All this manhandling and dotage doesn't fool me.
Nobody breaks you. All your buildings could be
washed in long muddy ropes through the mouths
of the sewers; still you would never be dissolved.
You have given suck to too many from your
fountain and your filigree; and that nipple in the mouth
imprints the nervous system.
Your filigree, spun from iron and crocheted
into amazing doorways, your fountain with its stone
curves gentle as a woman's shoulder move
in my bloodstream.

This realization dumbfounds me: That a neighborhood
parents us every bit as much as human parents do;
and nurtures in ways they can't. Grandfather, we have
been suckled at the same breast! It is in our blood to be
generous and to fashion order: Curve within curve
within square within circle, tight and perfect
like the act of love; to push aside the rubble and ashes
and raise up fountains—raise up fountains that love us.

## Shoes

I used to wear hard shoes,
shiny shoes with toe-points like needles
and tall narrow heels.
I used to wear fancy shoes,
all glitter or bits of mirror
with tiny bows and sparkling stones,
with millions of straps—like the movie stars.
I used to wear shoes to make me tall,
to lift me up, with soles of wood;
and everyone could hear me coming.
I used to wear fashion boots,
cover my calves in patent leather,
and make my ankles stiff as flagpoles.
I used to wear hiking boots with square toes,
with heavy soles that bit the ground,
that nothing could get through.
In those days, I walked looking straight ahead.
I didn't want to know anyone.
I kept my dangerous heart closed.

These days I wear shoes
with soles that hug the floor,
with toes open to the sun,
and heels open to the air,
plain shoes to gaze upon,
that cradle me as I come and go,
looking around the world.

Also, I have a dent in my hat.

## Florida Meditation

Blue veins in peach flesh
gripping a singing bamboo rake.
My father's strong warm hands
come back real to me
suddenly through a screen
at my younger brother's kitchen table.
The perfume of burning leaves,
like hot charred buttered toast,
serves me a quick yesterday
of Chicago fifty autumns past.
Checkered in black and white
and wool-wrapped, my father
rakes into a huge mound
bright broken pieces of 1940.
We plunge into them
before he sets them afire.

The old front yard returns.
My father made safe sanctuary
of that square.
Like some big German mother,
he combed the pale hair
and dark hard earth hide
of our plot of ground.
He fired a close comfort
with his nubby brown pipe.
Its thin blue line wavered
an upward spiral to meet
gangs of smoky ghosts
smoldering at our curb.
My father's kind broad back
and winking apple-wood pipe turned
the world into a top
that hummed, hummed for me.

Have you ever tried spinning
a top, making it stand?
Listen. This is important.
It needs to stand up only once—
humming, gleaming, singing
on its perfect point—
for us to know
such poise is a reality
and the very moment
that all things lean—yearn—toward.

Butter sheeted in a skillet dissolves
spontaneously into myriad beads;
and that's the same as feet,
back, hands, feelings simultaneously
intending the ball off the racquet's face.
And that's the same as
how the skier's downward lean
coincides perfectly with the snow pack.
And that's the same as one moment
one autumn afternoon
when my child's world hummed
a perfect circle of protection
of buttery burning leaves, tobacco,
my father's hands and pipe
and dear huge checkered frame
all spinning on a gleaming point.


(for A.J.)

## When you left home, Liz,

your young face set outward
and open as a sail, I sat down
to meditate upon your departure.
And first came this metaphor:
Out of the murky seaweed-tangle
of my bowels seventeen years
past appeared this perfect pearl,
rose-pink and rivered with pastel—
a daughter beautiful beyond speech.

Young womanhood came so soon.
And at some secret life-signal
(and despite all here that had been
wrong, broken or blown apart), with
light clear as a new day,
she gathered up her life and rolled
beautifully away.

Dusting, doing dishes, making beds,
preparing classes, that meditation
went on until it revealed to me
the secret wisdom in her then
that had refused to squander even a second,
but straightaway sought proper ground
to prepare to keep her promise
to life, and there clear a righteous space
to thrust down a fistful of roots
soon to shoot up the wonder of the green life-bud,
glowing and eager and fixed on flowering.

## High-Wire Walker

It's not as though you've never set foot
on a wire before;
but this time you must cross.
You know to trust your body
as helmsman,
your solar plexus
as rudder;
you've learned to use your arms
for balance
and that heart will take you
where muscle can't.

I give you ballet slippers
and help you put them on.
Your dad provides a safety line
and shyly slips a locket with "I love you"
into your hand. Sister Liz offers
her buff gloves smooth
as your own skin; brother Chris,
a winking pinkie ring.
Grandma Isabelle unfurls the parasol,
petal-pink and brilliant orange.

It's still early in the day.
Some few faithful friends
look on from hardwood benches.
Like the sun rising
horizon to noon,
your parasol describes a quarter arc,
horizon to directly above
the soft brown nest of your hair.
The tent is empty and quiet.
Your mind and eyes are in your legs.

No one suffers the dark,
dares the plunge,
balances against the fearsome wobble
of the heart
and the slow insistent downward pull
of fear
and comes back the same.

I watch the pink sun of your parasol
get tinier and tinier:
rising, setting; rising, setting.
You dare the dark on silver
somehow for us as well,
walk that filament alone
with all our thousand eyes alight
in the diamond points of your tiara
and sequins of your bodice.
Fear and joy in the same breath,
we watch you arch a pointed toe
over the shimmering wire
until your little sun hangs
a star,
far at the shadowed pole.

Next time and ever after,
you go out in concert with your peers.
Daybreak is an opening of parasols
and you have joined a conspiracy
of daring. My knee buckles
and I go off. Your arm will be
too short to grab my hair.
Your slipper sticks, free hand
churns the silken air.
Your God will catch you then
or pass you on.
I might not even see you fall.

So it is with us all.
High-wire armada,
we set out each dawn,
commanded by ghost compass,
braving whatever wind plucks
and plays our wire,
searching the dim distance
for the North Star.


(for Clare)

## Dancing with Fat Uncle Fergie


His hot heavy hand swallows
mine as the music starts. Dancing
with my fat Uncle Fergie is something
I hate. I shrink against the wall, shake
my head; but he laughs, pulls me
onto the floor where other couples pair up
for the downbeat. Then we're off.
It's always a polka or waltz. Round
and round, relentless. He huffs, clasping
me in his iron grip of joy, sweat flying,
while under the whirling ceiling,
the music drives us, separating the cells
of our bodies, washing in like a spring flood
to break me into islands held by centrifugal
force. This is how it always starts. But then
exhilaration pulls open mysterious pockets
in me to suck their contents out and I become
light, light, stepping, turning, stepping,
turning in all directions—all of us—above
the world, so high above the world.

## For Ira Progoff

1
the fierce strands binding
the fire caught within
the cocoon blazing
naked I run I run
my hair on fire
in my bowels
three stones burning

2
lump of clay
lump of life
at the threshold
in the doorway
a face lit
like the moon

3
The little child's bones
inside rattle and cavort,
play music when I walk.
The eros of the great engine
is their familiar; and how,
never sleeping, it draws
the juice along to force it
through the many narrows.
Again the ancient seeds
sprout in the collar of silt.
Oh, I am the holy child dancing
on the rim of the earth.
Forever is my name.

## A Wedding Poem

The mother of the groom daydreams that each of the three sisters
brings a lei to slip over the bride's honey-colored hair, to rest
on the red of her silk gown and over the groom's dark hair
and his dignified jacket. Instead, the minister closes the book—
the groom kisses the bride and everyone claps wildly.
In their vases, flowers burst open; flute and guitar
weave sprays of melody about each guest
and the lighted buildings of the city
stand taller along the boulevard,
along the river where it meets
the great gray spreading lake.
Pale gold champagne
begins to circulate.
The mother of the groom
observes the couple
tending well-wishers.
She thinks: How kindly
they return what
love itself gives
and thus restore
fresh promise
for the days ahead.
And so we raise our glasses
and take for our own
the fondest wishes of their hearts
and pledge to hold them fastly present
until each pushes forth its green shoot,
and drops the red and succulent fruit.

(for Chris and Fiona)

## A full moon

and it is the time of my menses.
The dead cells clot in the bright blood,
find their way through the dark passage.
Sometimes the will of my body to strip
and dislodge makes me cry out in agony.
It is horrible holding on like a drowner
against the torrent only to be torn away
piece by piece. Better to let go all at once
and become the corpse floating downstream.
It is when you find the readiness to be a dot
in the foaming whirlpool of yourself,
to lose sight there of all order and exist
as disintegration that you pass like a seed,
like the full moon, silently into the pool.

You tell me we cannot be the moon
because we ripple and breathe. It is true.
We are not the moon. We are the reflection
of the moon.

# III/ Scavenging

# Visit From a Maenad

Sometimes someone comes in the night
and pins you to the wall with her eyes
and a mute fear
overwhelms you.

You are not the same in the morning:
the floor cracks, the pot boils over.
spiders appear in the corners of the living room
making nests.

A dark inner road opens.
The imagination goes flying down it
barefoot—only to return puzzled about
why you do not go too.

You do not know how to go—
encumbered by your body,
laced to the linoleum
with hats and buttons and address books.

Somone comes in the night
to call you. You are
shocked to see your soul
already has its bags packed.

If you don't come
it will go without you
and there will be hell to pay
when you get the bills
from all over tarnation.

## Healing with Eidetic Images

You, a passerby, think me a common woman,
colorless, catching straw at my hem,
shifting the hardware of my days from hand to hand
and clutching about my shoulders like a shawl
tired remnants of the day's discarded promise.

But observe me more closely as I move nightward.
See at the threadbare places an unmistakable glimmer
or surprising flash of red, indigo or fire-yellow?
Does a common woman let such light or—listen—
walk in the midst of such soft singing?

## In a Man's Voice

These women always coming in here
with their stuff asking me,
      What should we do?
      What should we do?
How do I know what they should do?
They should stay at home or go out.
Whatever it is, they should do it
      themselves.
What do they want from me—
to be some camel to carry them
      across the desert
or a workman with a wheelbarrow
to make a monument out of that collection
they tote all day in their arms?
Don't they see that like them I am
      just a speck
      trying to hold on
      and not be
      blown away?
Don't they see it takes all my strength,
all my attention just to stay put
against this wind and awful heaving
      of the earth?
      Are they blind
      or made of stone
      that they keep asking
      for the impossible?

## Two soft lights

hover near her shoulders,
or now, about her head.
Do you see them?
Do you notice how
they never leave her,
move when she moves,
go where she goes?
So spirits can. Let's believe
she is the teacher they chose
from all eternity to learn
the lessons that come
from Mother Love,
that taproot from which all
love springs. They planned
bodies, but oh, do not need
them now. See how they draw
directly from her heart
the lessons of what holds
every earth, universe
and cosmos together.
Already the taste of a mother's
longings and desires for her children
fills their mouths, their bellies.
Later, perhaps, they will go on
into another life, but choose
also to stay. Let's believe spirits can.
Let's believe these stay to follow
her path, soft lights,
nourishing themselves
on that within her
which never stops,
falters nor fails;
on that which reaches
beyond death.

**Coyote**


he tells his family
paint the coyote
  the dove gray of spent hearth ashes
fray the grieving spindle of the neck
  just so
  the narrow chin pointing
  toward the moon
paint the moon a deeper gray
  make the sky black
  the moonlight muddied
like a damaged light pooling over bald rock
  the ragged coat and ears
  pouring down the cord of tail
make it your usual howling coyote picture
  except for the well-dressed crowd
  at the right
vertical in deep greens, rusts, chocolate browns
  huddled and stiff as wood
  backs turned
be sure the coyote's eyes
  are squeezed tight
  with a look that shows
this desertion lonelier than foraging
  and pull a long note with cutting edges
  through the tube of the howl
make it a reluctant departure
  a woeful climbing
  to the moon
and the coyote's voice
  extrude it from heart
  and spine together
make it tell those bodies carved from stone
  I would rather be hunted down
  by their cold blue steel
  than suffer this eternal wall of their backs
  I would rather be shot dead

**He says:**


the green fields flow through me
arms  breasts  stomach  become
a river of flowers
of grackles and white clouds
all my proud possessions
melt away
I open to the sky
sunlit  whispering
the tall grasses course through me
closing
there is no memorial
                but if you look up quickly
                you can wave


(for Joe Goubeaux)

## Early Morning at the Grotto:  November, 1943

The raised elbows. Helmets like turtle backs.
One squinting eye after another.
I see the captain's lips move, his arm reach
tall to unlock the snapping sounds,
tails of smoke, bits of glowing red, kangaroo kicks
at my chest. My mother's hand jerks loose.
My own body falls into rags about my feet.
The soldiers lower their guns. They bring
wheelbarrows to cart the corpses away.
We Jews track them to the steaming ditches
and watch them shovel: our murderers, who have
freed us to follow them everywhere.

## For RAWA
(The Revolutionary Association of the Women of Afghanistan)


We see your helmeted faces,
see you entombed in your gowns.
We see you cower with your children
under the bombs we drop, our bullets meant
to free you, instead destroying
what little you have. We can only feel
the terrible distance, my sisters.
We weep because we have failed—
failed you, failed ourselves; know
to have kept on would have prevented
this war, since it is women who create
and nurture common life. We do not permit
wars since they kill children and crops,
decimate families and the work of their hands;
nor do we tolerate the foolishness of cock fights.

We let ourselves slip back into the dream of men,
turned our gaze from the empowering mirror
to drink from his eyes the drugged wine
of his story and disappeared again ourselves,
leaving behind the fading markers of our work,
of all we had won and built and hoped to share
with you, our sisters far away and waiting.
Now you wake us with your cries.
We rub the deadly sleep from our eyes.

## That Intruder, Death

slips into your bed,
twines its fingers through your hair
and breathes into your ear
a sound so soft and familiar
you don't even know you've left home.

## Your Life Fit You Like Too-Tight Boots

Last night you pulled out, grunting and sweating
through the moment when it wouldn't come off
and wouldn't go back. Then the little easing,
> the ankle relaxing
> its argument,
> the heel its hold;
> then the little movement
> of slipping
> into freedom.


Your life held you too tight, like an angry fist.
You slid out of its grip, escaped under the arch
> where the little finger curls,
> leaked out between the knuckles
> and evaporated like sweat.


Unknot your wings, then for the breakaway.
Flame into the bright blue. Let us hear
you scream joy at your release.
> The air will be scarred
> by the heat of your flying.
> And we will not forget
> you were here.

# Dateline Deerfield

In Deerfield, the young man with everything to live for,
the young man home on vacation from Harvard with a
straight A average and an enviable summer opportunity at
the well-known law firm of Hinkley, Cardy, Hammersmith
and Leland; the handsome young man with a little red
MG of his own and scores of friends who had come up
with him from Hardy Prep and who, like him, were doing
very well, as everyone expected, and who would go to
Europe, of course, like him, the summer after next, and
whose grandmothers and grandfathers, like his, had lived
in these same towns and whose names are known at banks
and on boards of trustees at colleges and universities and
museums; the young man with a pedigree as long as
your arm and who is always so accommodating playing
doubles at the Racquet Club took the dainty Japanese
revolver with the jade and ivory handle—the one his
father had given his mother three years before and about
which she had exclaimed, "Oh, I don't know how I could
ever pull the trigger, even if I had to!" and emptied it
into his parents (she rising up with his name on her lips
from the pillow and then slumping forward over the satin
sheets, and the father taking four bullets in his large belly
at the foot of the mother's bed where he had run, shock
still set on his face when they turned the body over the
next day), rifled the safe in the floor of the den, threw a
suitcase onto the luggage rack of the little red MG and
squealed from the garage below the palatial bedroom
with its scents of fine veneer and jasmine bath powder
and the two stilled bodies; and thought, speeding away
through the black night, sweat clammy on his brow, his
heart faster and louder than his engine, that he'd had no
choice in the matter—it had clearly been a case of kill or
be killed.

## Do You See These Dark Threads?

They do not, as you might think, speak of the end,
but mark the middle years. The fabric of every life
has this dark streak for its center. It is here the colors
all come together before they are separated out again.
It is a trying time in the weaving. The thread knots
and curls; and it is hard to see differences with all
the values flattening out. A special alertness is called for,
an extended concentration and faithfulness to the art
of the process. But it will be a wonder when it is finished.

This is my middle, my dark streak. I work it
with all the skill I have. I believe in faithfulness
and in art. If I can't see how it is coming along
because I must attend it so closely, I trust
all to harmonize. My love of the work has
not changed my whole life. Love has its own store
of learning that guides the general body
when fingers falter or focus fails.

You wait in the gray, seeing a mad woman
at her loom. You wonder if I will ever stop
to eat or stir the fire. You have long since
given up the hope of a meal yourself. I know
you are there, in the shadows. I do not speak,
weaving, weaving. You wait against the wall.
If you should decide to leave, I would remain
at my bench; but without you, I would
work in a cold room,
a cold room.

## Grace

Again must death tread
my hallways and confront
me from corners until I open
my arms to it wide as I did
to you who, despite private preferences
of where to sleep and what to eat,
what to chase down or leave alone,
never found me wanting in anything
serious, took me as is, folded yourself
into my days, found my ways comely
and interesting, my preoccupations
curious and acceptable, my presence
home.

Now will toll, will toll your absence.

And how, caught off guard, can my heart
bear the forming of every shadow
into your shape, the hearing of any muffled rustle
as the shifting of your body, each small high note
as speech freeing itself from your throat?
How will I stop from calling your name
as I come through the door, explain
your absence to the walls, the philodendron
and shamrock? How will I explain to the sunlight
climbing through the window intent on licking
the butterscotch of your face, lighting
the tortoise shell of your ears, sprawling
the rust, black and brown saddle of your back,
losing itself in the pure down of your bib
that you have disappeared? And when it searches
this place and cannot find your exquisite body,
how will I explain to the face of its grief
that you are gone forever?

And how will I comfort this air?

# IV/ THE LONG IRIDESCENT FLIGHT

## In my early-morning mind

                                I invite you
to Sunday breakfast. But you must bring
your own coffee; I have the milk and sugar.
I set the foldout table on the back porch
so you can keep company with treetops
and watch against the blue sky the tiny flag
of the Edgewater Beach Apartments snap
in the wind. A linen cloth for the table. A bowl
of pansies. The bulging Sun Times. Bacon
and provolone for the omelet. I'm good
with eggs. A little strawberry yogurt, fat
baking powder biscuits, butter and honey
and marmalade. What have I left out?
Oh, the early June air teasing our hair.
A slow rumbling bumblebee. The great tree
to the right that throws high her umbrella
under which we can talk, read and spread
butter on another biscuit. Your eyes stray
across my neighbor's yard to rest upon her iris,
daisies and just-sprouted corn. You let your hand
fall softly to finger a comment onto my cat winding
through the legs of your chair. At the end, stepping
from the clutter of dishes, you kiss me your thanks.
It is your way, though I am already thanked and can
hardly stand, become so drunken now from the sight
and smell of you so near. You wave your way down
the back and I follow your hand, the top of your head,
the striking of your boot heels, then the arcing squeak
of the gate. I wait while all that space washes clean
again, but without you. I feel the longing dig through
me as I turn in my bed and begin again. It is Sunday.
I invite you to breakfast. You must bring your own coffee.

## Under the fur of moss

in the moist breath of fallen leaves
and blue bodies of lakes,
among giant stones
and through thick stands of trees
my love will search you out,
and find you too in the city,
in the girth of a man's hand,
the soft unfolding of an arm,
in the spaces between bodies.

Somewhere your music plays.
The sleek silken energy
directs it like wind over water,
like wind over sand. Your pure note draws me
like sun glowing through a single leaf;
and all my cells open their doorways of light
and you will not be able to say no.
Somewhere your music plays.
The faithfulness of my heart will find it.

And I will gather into me your body of beauty.
In your eyes I will see rivers and mountains,
beaches, meadows in your open face.
Your body will touch mine with green woods,
with white caps, with the peace of snow.
Your breath of God will bring to me
the flow of water, currents of molecules,
rivulets of air laced with wild flowers,
with the scent of animals and rain on hot stones.

I float on that slipstream of light we share
until your sacred darkness opens and I let go
to sink into your holy quiet thick with kindness,
thick with mystery, sink into this firmament
of all you are, apparent and hidden, into this
elemental sky where the gems of your goodness

greet me here and here with their soft radiance.
I will search faint ripples there until one bestirs
itself with power and gathers into a will.

At once we come together, fire into fire,
wind into wind, until there is but one
form caught on itself. Or we, fishermen,
have hooked the fish we trolled for within
one another, a beauty of fresh knowing
we breath out of the organ of our joining,
watch it shimmering into that consciousness
out of which we too are born, its note
clear and uncompromised.

By now we have spawned a little school
like a scattering of bells or string of stars.
Each with its blessing undulates backwards
and falls like a pebble into us to mark forever
the soft bodies of our beings and lodge there
like a prehistoric insect caught in clay,
or like spoor encapsulated in a bead of amber.
Such strikes to our awareness sink, feather,
and turn to satin, etched into our becoming.

You will take the knowing which this marking is
to your place eons away and let your teachers
there absorb the pleasure of its figure
through their fingertips. I go with you in my part,
and carry this marking here too where its signal
blesses a thousand souls as I pass along Belmont,
along Halsted, on Fullerton. And you come with me,
your part being also of me, Master of Locks,
Healing Stone, Beloved.

## Let me come to you as Lady Moon

                        on bare feet
above tree tops, across dark waters.
In these mists, among whispering veils,
let me find you where you are closeted.
Let me steal through the window,
on tiptoe cross your floor.
Let me slip between your sheets
in my cool and luminous body
to draw you from your dreams.
Let me bring to you, O my prince,
my husband, in the quiet
of this summer's night,
the exquisite music of love.

## Moving Between the Flakes

I know you are just a humble man:
you are wood, are leather scarred
and worn to a shine. I am
a simple woman, myself,
and love a round-edged stool,
a hand-made spoon, a fruit-bearing bowl.
I hear singing in such things.

It is snowing, beloved:
Black crows against black branches;
the love of the snow sifting
between. We belong too
in this picture as a part of Nature
moving between the flakes.

## I enter you like mist

like smoke, like fog or clouds.
And so you also enter me,
that light of dawn just before dawn.
We kiss and that kiss is a continuum
like a slow-moving river threading
space. Behind it, under it, is music.
Or the music is the slow-moving river,
or the river is the music and the kiss;
or the kiss is the river and the music
and we two as one, slow-moving as clouds
upon the bosom of heaven.

## Between the hills

is a valley
of plates of earth divided,
forested and folded. I wait there
to see you coming, slow
and deliberate, over the rise,
carrying all that earth does,
carrying its spirit. I open my arms
wide, around us the world in song.
We retreat to our secret place,
one of rocks old and smooth that resolve
into the floor of a deep cave. Here,
while nature holds us in her arms,
we open our hearts and bodies
to speak all that we are and all
that we desire in the language of love.
Nature protects us, for our coupling is
her heartbeat pulsing the mystic blood
to other lovers in other caves murmuring
in embrace and circulating it back
into the fields, oceans and mountains
to flying and crawling creatures—
our brethren all—anxious now,
watching the distant rise
for the sight of the beloved.

## Let us curl up, love

in a leafy shadowed nest
deep in the silence of the woods.
God is so big we cannot find Him,
but we can find each other.

## Each morning I bathe

rinse my hair with water of violets
or white lilac; for I never know
where I might come upon him.
I must be ready should he step
through the great gate, round
a corner of the gallery, or be
found at his ease, sipping
sake with other men and telling
tales. To speak to him it is not
permitted; but I can lean near to fill
his cup or offer a delicacy, and let
my fragrance fill his body
and his mind. Having no
ambition but this, I can be
patient, and a thousand ways
enter him before he wakes
into my arms. Each night I light
the lantern by my bed, my lord.
Come soon.

## We Are Smoke-Gray

long and thin

        satin skinned

rub

        bellies and breasts

raise up

        fire

open our mouths

        hungry for one another

I swallow you

        you swallow me

we are

        smoke-gray

single-celled

        with a single black eye

swim

     in the body of God

## Among the tall bright flowers

we sit close

you cover my hands
with your hand

my heart quiets
our peace becomes deep

there is nothing
we cannot give to one another

## It is as if we had fallen asleep


dreamed seven hundred years
        of separate lives
hurrying past like flocks of geese,
        like a sky full of wings,
or like underground water
        over stones,
until finally we flowed like diffused light
        into these bodies
to wake to the daybreak
        of one another.

Again, the meeting of eyes,
        the brush of fingers
as we lift the spindle laid aside
        our last life together.
Again to spin the common stuff,
        the ebb and flow of feeling,
that filament we shuttle at the loom
        to work at the pattern weaving us.
Seven hundred years have not blurred
        this design imprinted in our blood.

We pick at ham and grapes,
        taste strawberries and fresh milk.
The old sun spills through the open door;
        we laugh together, let it soak our feet.
As we chew the friendly gossip of the day,
        you reach over bread crumbs, the yellow cloth,
to take my hand; far below our talk
        a silent conversation moves
and we begin again to fold into one another,
        like ribbons of an ancient river plaiting.

We will dream another stream of lives.
I know not when we will wake
nor where we will appear.
But letting go now into your eyes
my threads scatter like straws.
I find your petal softness
weaving into me,
And all my cells take on
the color of your fragrance.

# EPILOGUE

## The Crows

### I

My dear, our crows are out again.
Yesterday, as I left for work,
I saw them side by side on a branch
of that tall tree in Mr. Lompoc's yard,
their hunched bodies two hearts in silhouette.
They still keep neighborhood with us, though we are
in the dog days of winter with snow eight feet high
and swords of Damocles that hang from porches and gutters.
The alley with its ruts covered has become a confusion
I must negotiate with firmness of purpose
and humility, but holding to my course; otherwise
my car's grill ends up through somebody's fence.

### II

I am in the dog days of winter,
feelings storming or in a freeze for weeks.
I can only bow to the will of the weather
and go forward on small feet. My last shamanic journey,
my path for this next while looked like my alley.
The job, I was told, was to keep moving.
Each day I climb into my boots, pull my hat low
and, like the crows, hunch against the weather, sit
in whatever storm is out there, learn its language,
accommodate its humor and shape until I discover
that somehow even the beast I fear most transmutes
into blossoms under the magic of its own will for good.

III

You sit with me waiting for winter to pass.
Soon the sun will come climbing past
the clouds, the buildings begin to drip
and the soil grow spongy and green.
We will feel the long breath of spring river
beneath our bodies and make us fluff
our feathers, pick and preen; then spread
our wings, deliberate, and, in a symphony
of ease, lift off, flashing sapphire, diamond and rose.

Zoe Keithley is a native of Chicago transplanted to Sacramento, where she teaches workshops, edits, and hosts public fiction readings. In Chicago she taught writing at Columbia College while earning a Master of Arts in the Teaching of Writing and a Master Teacher certificate in the Story Workshop® approach to writing. She also writes novels, short stories, and children's stories.